Sanctuaries of the Beer Years

Sanctuaries of the Beer Years

Some Poems

MAX ENOS

RESOURCE *Publications* · Eugene, Oregon

SANCTUARIES OF THE BEER YEARS
Some Poems

Resource Publications
An Imprint of Wipf and Stock Publishers
199 W. 8th Ave., Suite 3
Eugene, OR 97401

www.wipfandstock.com

PAPERBACK ISBN: 978-1-5326-9779-1
HARDCOVER ISBN:978-1-5326-9780-7
EBOOK ISBN: 978-1-5326-9781-4

Manufactured in the U.S.A.   11/26/19

This book is dedicated to Joan Fitzgerald O'Hara

Contents

I. NEW ENGLAND

An actual poem.

Descent of snowlight

There was a New Year's 2013

What the winter hides

Emerson Inn

Tavern floor, bartender's moment

Now, Here

Unsaved at Ralph's Diner

Feeling pretty good for four hours of sleep

Worries in Worcester (Paris of the 80s)

Night visit

Magnolia

Gypsy Bar

Lighthouse swing

What the wind mulls

Fuck this poem entitled, "After delivering your mail"

Meditation on the color wine

Remnants

For one about to reach her beginning's end

Leaving Salisbury

II. SEOUL

For Ana (if we're being dishonest)
Second time waking in Asia
In private, at a public wall
Our neighborhood, 은행 사거리
Starting again
In Seoul, a sight of perseverance
Another cute ending
Midnight walk, wet October night
American soldier in Seoul
Snow on a steep mountain
Five p.m. twilight darkenings
Snow & sickness
The coffee remaining
Don't know crows from ravens
Coffee & quietude at the Anguk MMCA
Nervous, intelligent brewing
April in Seoul
Remote cafe in Nowon-Gu
Acid rain disposition
In the sunlight on Buram Mountain 불암산
Watching the night-hikers from Erik's far-off porch
Wild cat at 9 p.m.

III. NEW ENGLAND *II*

Safe haven

Quiet hour

Resolves at twenty-five resolved at thirty-five

In harborside barlight

Cannot remember

Driving to ADK to crash the Kozowski 4th of July

Portsmouth day

This shit town

Did the dog just make that noise?

Same: Kilim coffee walk in the snow

Winter Scene

Currier and Ives

(your snowstorm morning lips)

Portsmouth iv

Cabot St. Market when it's pouring

April Fools, not what no one talks about

I'm a part of the night

Berkshires return

Without a forgotten line

Debris by the tracks

K.

In Rockport's last light, evening is palpable, has breath.

Acknowledgments

Thank you Lynne and Rod for everything, Deirdra, Kristen for unending support and love, my mentor Sue Standing, Mary Riso for guidance, readers Roxy Azari and Alex Freiberg, and my idiot friends.

I

New England

AN ACTUAL POEM.

Time: When stars fade from sight   Light: Lighthouse light becoming less stark
By: The dark barklines
Through: Illumined fog from the woods, the sea?
What: That's tough. There are morning dogs mid-shout in houses shaken
by a dawn train
    which transports coal as its engineer
       sips dark, dark coffee and
          resigns to a circuitous life
            as a moth flutters to her coffee-damp lips.
Why?

DESCENT OF SNOWLIGHT

What is there to believe
when, at first sight, love leaves?
On the window, an oneiric frost transmigrates the day's thoughts.
Scent of autumn's death dances raw,
sunflower of the moon,
as thawed candles burn and mute pumpkins pray submission.

In such a rout coldsnap,
there is a communal stiffening, stem to petal.
The radiator sputters, cranks, blows.
Magnolia petals, once tender-silk, toughen and quiver over its heat.
 Take me
from this mill-lined city of Kerouac
and phantom industrialists
and I'll forgive everyone, everywhere, of everything.

THERE WAS A NEW YEAR'S 2013

One pub crawl from lunacy or delirium tremens,
    streaks of Nashua's lamp-lined lunar streets, state-border blur.

There was a commute to the Lowell Treatment Center
    on a dry, stop-at-the-gas-station morning.
Route 40 coffees and consumerisms, morning scratch tickets
    and a 7:30 a.m. moon to genuflect the total morning—hot thoughts
of more coffee
    over the iced Merrimack, limacine there
under a thin, shivering bridge
    and the simple sun rising,
blinding, binding.

WHAT THE WINTER HIDES

Worcester in its dusk presents a variegated view of endless triple-deckers.
Worcester, where roofs are dripping, smells of petrichor.
On Ormond Street, mounds of peppered snow vanish.
Resounding crickets surround the Armenian Church of the Martyr.
A bird surveys the concurrency of drying and melting.
It was, after all, the longest winter.
Forgotten was the true width of the sidewalk,
how fog travels after warm rain,
and how calm porch-talks can saunter
at night across this Wormtown Americana.
A woman smokes on her deck, thin lips pressed west—
your guess, good as my guess.

EMERSON INN

Does it stitch, suture,
or tell a sutra
in which I am a granddad mouse
with plum-stained fur?
Things for which I do not care.
Save me or spare me
from this silence astir.

TAVERN FLOOR, BARTENDER'S MOMENT

Boots tap by cashews unswept, peel off stale ales spilled
as foolish air rushes in from the tavern door.
Men return from a smoke
this time smelling of coke
and cane and smoke and rain
and prepare to resume errant passes at the bartender.
They will continue the mental liquidation of their work week
against the start of hers.
She pours their value in pity and disdain.
Trials, lusts, attempts,
all for draught.

NOW, HERE

It's a steep trip to midnight
during a fresh air break outside The Met
listening to Eric Bolton's band
(forget their new name)
cover Juicy or King Lear, can't hear
all that well in this stabbing rain.
Cars pass, flash headlights in such post-twilight rain
optical stains soon to spawn my third migraine this month
minutes from here, miles from nowhere.

UNSAVED AT RALPH'S DINER

No one here likes Springsteen.
    They all have kids and tattoos.
No one here, even in the privacy of a home, dances, moves, moans.
A hip, rude bartender (former student)
(in the resonance of some neo-Ramones and mind-dulling privilege)
    gives me a drink like a good little lostboy.
I leave my tip in the palpable New England nothingness of this diner-turned-bar.
Time to go. Why? Why not? Got to go groan, be alone,
be left alone
    by the people I've hounded.

FEELING PRETTY GOOD FOR FOUR HOURS OF SLEEP

The hill's autumnal winds, final green leaves, cider and pumpkin stands.
Where does it end?
    Neruda and Bradbury in the newfound 7 p.m. darkness.
    7 p.m. darkness! Where did James Taylor
and Tanglewood on 4th of July go?
On which eternal jetty is July napping?
Where am I, drunk
beneath Berkshire stars
    aged 23 searching for age?
    I must find July, wake it
    take it for granted once more.

But suddenly I feel all right for four hours of sleep.
Directions change, harbor winds rise, die,
and confused college sophomores spill off Highland Street
into twilights, limelights, toward books and deadlines.
Coffee cups leak silently in their libraries.
Scholars journey through their 20s, before the 2020s, ready to roar again.
Caffeine will hit us all street-side at noon.
I will get another coffee.
It will be too late.

WORRIES IN WORCESTER (PARIS OF THE 80s)

Another night with the moon somewhere behind hillside triple-deckers
somewhere hiding, perhaps playing dice, necking
or whistling its old, blue tune.

Another night searching
for the moon
between city buildings.

Another night's attempt at sleep
the teacher worries
about his troubled students, fast asleep.

NIGHT VISIT

Charles Olson and I skip rocks, dark moths
which kiss fish across the harbor's top
    until swallowed in Lethe darkness.

Chuck knows more about allusion than I care to know about anything.
What I like about him: He isn't in New York
but Gloucester.
He claims his rock skipped half-a-dozen times. Seemed like more.

And there's no minor poets, no major figures, he says. Only breath.
Says he's written a handful of poems since death
then asks about me.

MAGNOLIA

The sky earlier
could have been painted and titled
Yellow Death
Ephemeral Love
90s Gauze
    Mellow Birth, or
Petty Crows
all of you.

GYPSY BAR

just give me back youth and I promise to stop writing.
though, in this country of concession, a warm sanctuary may suffice.
make it a bar above which I can live and sleep and dream.
light the bar gold like a beehive in which I may hide, where sins renew
or are invented.
line the Mt. Rushmore of drinkers against the back wall
in the fleeting lighthouse light
to be illumined like the front line of some wartime pantomime.
hang a portrait of a dogged fisherman
to watch our sweaty, bohemian toasts to life and darkness.
in perpetual booze, we drip
with life and darkness.

LIGHTHOUSE SWING

In darkness, the lighthouse light swings over the course of obsidian ocean
and sweeps the coastal road
down to where you breathe.
Light will leave.
What are you watching at sea?
Light stings endless water and returns
to stir nocturnal half-blinking bush cats.
Who, there, stands
under wirecrows
in the stalk of your shadow, being?

WHAT THE WIND MULLS

is what leaning lips seek
    on certain foggy afternoons in Gloucester
        where there are more hours in a day
        than a clocking tic or ticking
        clock may infer, and where bony fingers bend
        over unhinged doors that belong
        to creatures who know
        clockmakers who know time
is also what the breeze hides
    in the guise of grass, now mustard in hillside sway

FUCK THIS POEM ENTITLED,
"AFTER DELIVERING YOUR MAIL"

This effusive welcome at the door
by old friends, decaying intellectuals
is one I saw coming when I was 22. I'm 31
or so. They pose and
spout nervous nothings while rigid bracelets dangle.
The door to their new brownstone
is brown. I must admit
they've made it.
They've made it here
at least. This is where their kid
will grow to be five
or six before they move to a farther layer of Greater Boston.
The other men at this function are wearing what you could call
"restrained comfort" clothing—I don't know. I don't know about any of it.
I don't know how to format something so shitty. So unpoetic.
I showed up in my USPS uniform
having come from WORK and all.
I'm bitter. I'm bitter they work on their own terms
and I work on their terms as well.
Well, we're not being honest at this party
or I'd tell Keith, by the chips, that he's a sellout for his corporate contract.
These people—they're all
what their parents would call successful.
Men calculate beards, go through motions.
Women occupy vacant eyes.
Fingertips hover mechanically
over one another's shoulders. Vowed possessions in this serpentine room.
I grow impatient and let out too-loud of a sigh.
They see it as a foray.
These seem like people who, when their child is 11,
about the time they start voting—well, never mind.
I don't know shit. I'm here and I did this to myself.
I swallow as I enter a new room.

These are supposed to be my friends
but I can't respect any of these people except for Lily there
sitting on the heater. She's in a union too,
and nods patiently in the spindrift of some lawyer's wind.
He quite considers his clean life interesting.
She sees me for a second.
We're perhaps the only single people left in Boston.
I doubt she'll ever look at me again.
Some savage, early-20s spirit possesses me and I yell, irreparably,
"Chahlie, where's the fahkin' beer?"
I want a beer.
I don't have a Boston accent, but that's how it is said.
I'm looked at like a loiterer, a distasteful animal.
My hatred grows towards them all. Couple A,
together since 19, guided tours and Islamophobia, now they're engaged. Couple B,
addicted to relationships, mistake routine for love. Couple C,
an apartment with degrees on the wall of an unused office, wooden floors
and corporate jobs "only until I pay off my loans." I thought this might happen
to my friends.
In Boston, distracted by changing seasons, distracted
by dinner parties and social humble brags . . .
(but no previous generation was all that different, all that innocent;
a proclivity to settle, embrace apathy, fear death, entertain ennui, enjoy complacency,
all this, on the first day of fall).

MEDITATION ON THE COLOR WINE

Autumn spills in every conceivable morbid direction.
Wine glasses have their own hour of foliage
as colorless green vases, wobbly on stone-cool garden tables, are full of ideas
yet asleep, in an increasingly furious and red nighttime mist.
September sighs
having heaved one final heatwave
and will offer no more foliage, as in old days,
no, all falls fast now, dry and brownish
    like a feeling of loss
      felt through two lifetimes.

REMNANTS

Tides are such fetid and impersonal natures
when there are memories on this beach
in which you still sleep, sweeping sea at our feet,
scent of sodden dogwood washed ashore,
and transparent spiders dashing.
Your hair was long, and I remember it
One: White in the cold moon's frostlight.
Two: Bourbon, tangled with an afternoon sun,
one with the earth, then static
as if skies try to pry you
while waves dampen your cheeks, icy sleek in such lighthouse light
long-reaching shadows
casting negatives across your pearl face.

You became meerschaum on dark sands.
Were you always slipping down rivulets of sand into the sea?
Bit by bit, your memory wears at me.
Three: Ashes of hair, lips
adrift with ancient seaweed and the Hesperus.
Old Garden and the steel ocean smooth beyond comprehension.
Are you beheld by blue stars?

    I held you once, too.
    I do not agree with your dying decree.
I tremble to spill you to quiet waves, moon's wrinkled visage
my own, to depths to descend or disperse.
I retrace our hundredfold hollow footprints
sand-scribed names, washed
and rewashed anonymously by high-tides whose times we knew.
We knew that for one of us
it would begin like this.

FOR ONE ABOUT TO REACH HER BEGINNING'S END.

Nothing is truly owed or deserved,
owned or preserved. Simply sit
and contemplate the destruction,
the air, the sudden rain
constructing puddles. Learn
how to sip coffee, read about crisis. Note
    how crisis can evolve like odor
then disappear unnoticed.
Next, my friend,
be wary the distinguished man;
question his years.

LEAVING SALISBURY

In a garden of golden dunes
behind scarves and scars
to eastern seas, she spoke
with eyes at ease, of hope
a soul unwebbed, in ebb
with the westerly breeze.
Ready to traverse damp, dark country
to be where a new tide moves
like marmalade, smooth
under sanguine moonlight, waiting.

II

Seoul

FOR ANA (IF WE'RE BEING DISHONEST)

I.
We're in the twilight of our mime-like lives
wherein your skin becomes your own skin
in the dim grail of that city-night window.
Our shadows, new moon waves upon the amber wall, waver in abstraction.
Under the gaslight, our gazes engage (feigned devotions).
The utterances are convoluted moonwild whispers
lost to the midnight chamber of memory.
Your dreamcatcher earrings, stripped,
lay tangled on the nightstand
and fail to sort what's haunted.
Your smoked voice, dahlia ennui,
stiffens as you yearn or yawn.

II.
But we share only what comes next.
We share silence.
Here have been conscious outtakes.
Tonight, yellow lights beyond
my studio in Seoul
silence.
You are in Boston, the first fallen leaf pinned in your hair.
A nightjar at noon,
I wouldn't recognize your voice in the darkest room.

SECOND TIME WAKING IN ASIA

6 a.m. in Seoul I breathe in sighs.
I try to live ascetically.
I live apologetically.

IN PRIVATE, AT A PUBLIC WALL

Was it the monotony? I search to forget you
outside the walls of Deoksugung Palace.

OUR NEIGHBORHOOD, 은행 사거리

A late and spontaneous walk.
A night I'd had a glass of red, glass of white, you know
and it had rained but the humidity hadn't had its death.
In those days, there was that park by 7/11
and a cafe, condensation on its Hangul windows.
There were puddles to hop over.
My solitude was
disturbed when I ran into you, 2 a.m.
    exiting WA Bar with our friends. *I wish now were then.*
It was the day North Korea launched a third nuclear test.
We laughed it off and later you fell asleep on your couch
while the others played cards until 6 a.m.
but at 3 a.m.
when we were still in darkness
and I was still new to Korea, that expat community,
I looked for a look. You are careful; no. It's not that.
Never would you
send eyes to tell me—No.
I looked
in vain, I know.
We drank and shuffled while on the couch you slept.
I had my questions.
The contrast in beauty was apparent.

STARTING AGAIN

be brief and soft and
do not smell of anything to distract.
touch
where hair meets neck. only
touch. do not hold, grab—just
mean it. no kisses of the past matter.
soft, slow, brief
because when
with lids closed
are brown eyes brown?
the smiling silence after.
(how we always say funny words between kisses and sometimes
we go weeks between kisses
and I want to because I miss you.
I haven't missed anyone ever
and I presume that if kissing did not exist
we would easily discover it)

IN SEOUL, A SIGHT OF PERSEVERANCE

Is it young lovers' zeitgeist, or just people
wanting to own,
                be owned?
All the twenty-somethings peck, hold, grab,
pose, act, overreact.
But is it better in Boston
where no one believes in love?
    That shit city bred a resignation, an affinity for settling down.
Boston needs mountain-lore.
On mountains scattered throughout Seoul
are middle-aged ringless swingers
who swig makgeolli and send laughs down to the city.
Boston
should have some of what they're having,
but Boston
doesn't even allow happy hour.

ANOTHER CUTE ENDING

I digress. The moths have been dead and born again in the months since you wrote
and I've been silent.
I'm a moth-ridden overcoat, a torn moth-wing among your
monarch spread. I should go rot
in some warehouse mothy cardboard box.

Are you looking for a body to displace,
    to watch you grow sadder?
I have my anxieties.
You told me about your mother's Do*toevsky collection last time we spoke
and you looked forward to my letters.
    Well, here I am, in another foreign country
using the same language to express my ineptitude
using the same excuses to express my negligence.
I swear I can still be genuine.
I swear I'm capable of avoiding a cute ending to this late-September letter.
In fact, I wrote you a letter *and* a postcard.
Is it worse that I didn't make an effort to send them?
That I didn't hover over the postbox contemplating their significance?
For my own part, I think I will.

MIDNIGHT WALK, WET OCTOBER NIGHT

Look through the darkness at the ivy bushes
    past the secret grief of city dogs
    to stray cats, perfect in moonless wanderings.

Find corporeal yearning and primal fear
    in the presence of Buram Mountain
    a mountain past its midnight.

Come into the shanty neighborhood
    where restless delivery boys smoke in dark alleys
laugh and lean against mopeds
    and tell tales of sex while sending texts tinged with love and lust.

Feel the cigarette ends of husbands, wet with October night
    stepping into business suits
    thirty minutes since . . .

Walk into an ill-lit GS25 contemplating your tired relationship.
    Buy tasteless coffee, then walk some more
along the path of glowing cat-eyes
to where the rest is happening now.

AMERICAN SOLDIER IN SEOUL

— Yet to learn "hello" in Korean
"war" tattooed in Kanji
— been here a year
runs from fear to fear
— buys Jingu, my love, roses
and whispers at grade-six level
— levels me
with a fist
— I could
be wrong

SNOW ON A STEEP MOUNTAIN

    I envy snow on a steep, grassy mountain
full of shadows, ledges and stairways leading to cinnamon clouds.
    I envy stillness
as my young hangover declines on the way to mountainside batting cages
as somewhere, someone
begins stacking my cairns.

FIVE P.M. TWILIGHT DARKENINGS

It's the week before December 25th.
Smoke and a white cross pierce the gray forsaken sky.
Seoul City grows among us, glows before us.
Lights take a stand against the advancing night
and rooftop trees disappear beneath the green-white mountain.
The city grows among us, keeps growing, long
long beyond the time
our own groaning is up.

SNOW & SICKNESS

We're all lonely and dying
but isn't it nice to read a poem about it?
I'd been bed-ridden and worried about my ailments,
nerved and disturbed, when Heena texted me.
She's suffering from migraines too.
"It's snowing!" Her simple sentence
packed with beauty
brought me out of my loft
down to the window. The snow was beautiful.
Sometimes it's that simple.
I questioned whether I'd enjoy it again in good health.
I went out
to feel it.
In the street, the kids were making large snowballs.
I envied their health.
Korean citizens hustled around holding umbrellas beneath the whiteness,
general throughout all Seoul.
My Ma's card arrived while I was away from the office-tel.
With snow in my hair, I went to get tea
to write about it all.
Tea
because I was sick.
I'd been sick for months.
The porch of Darin Cafe is a motif. The rickshaw
with damp cardboard, hoarded by the homefree, is also a motif.
But this poem
was done six months later, still sick.
All those years we thought we were dying,
we were dying.

THE COFFEE REMAINING

Keep this coffee unfinished.
Pouring coffee is pouring hope, you know
and when it's gone, well, then
I'm just a man wishing he had more.
Merely a guy
sitting by an empty mug.
Ah, look: She, who was smoking,
has returned
smelling of smoke, seeking more mud.
(music drowns in this chatter)
The cold-faced barista lets out a laugh.
It is not warm outside, if you wished to know,
and last night I gave my first rim job.

DON'T KNOW CROWS FROM RAVENS

Are these crows or ravens
who dare break the bare mountain's winter silence
and caw us into spring?
I know nothing of birds nor love poems.
Mountain hawks, if such a thing, stir clouds under a jaundice sun.
An austere temple is concealed among thin trees.
Where are the leaves? There's one: fall's remainder,
lost among seasons.
I know that I will soon go to work
then I will drink
    then I will repeat.
(I only hope in this one clear moment to solidify the memory of when you,
con-artist extraordinaire, surprised me
on the peeling stone steps descending from Bottle Bar into the gloom of central
Itaewon
[snow forming] with a confident kiss in confidence)

COFFEE AND QUIETUDE AT THE ANGUK MMCA

Middle school romances or contemporary art exhibitions,
    which has more value?
This wind upends umbrellas, rips thorns from flowers, tousles a schoolboy's hair.
The rain destroys dreams of a day spent in the park.
The Gyeong Palace walls are wet and dark
and trees spill rain onto that cold iron table.
I [i like this area in the rain] return to a wooden teahouse craft brewery
alone, a sip of americano, a dash of Americana,
and there's still hope. Mountain backdrop.
Artists walk through other artists' galleries.
Dark branches flow like veins in the gray sky.
Petals, slower than rain, fall
like prenatal memory
from some flowers, at home, in Asia.

NERVOUS, INTELLIGENT BREWING

Two baristas distinguish themselves from ghosts of baristas past.
Stoic face, trembling hand, she reviews the menu
written 2 a.m. the night prior. The night prior. . .
Her hair is tied back, black.
Deeper-yet, she considers her menu (fonts, spacing, coloring, texture).
The other barista is serious too, but has laughed once and now begins to clean
stretching an arm—yawning athlete of coffee!—to collect forsaken mugs.
Well, they could be sisters, lovers, business partners
who knows anything except that this is their decided craft.
With precision and peering intent:
every drip, word, bean
every filter is calculated.
Hours of scholarship
to be ready for the perfect cup
to hear people declare: "Best Coffee in the City"
Today, on their sidewalk, in green and blue chalk, their coffee-of-the-day is twice:
과테말라 또는 *SHB* 안티구아
Guatemala, or SHB Antigua.

APRIL IN SEOUL

April is cancelled. Was it skipped?
April is no longer the old April
but some vague, late-May.
Rarely rainy, migraines all the same,
feeling dispossessed, stressed, male, lame, tame,
displeased, teased by all light,
disinterested, feigned, and slightly sick.
Whatever this is, it's deeply ingrained.
Might be mere boredom, the highest of all privilege.

REMOTE CAFE IN NOWON-GU

Something of the thin tree's branches,
severed for the sake of city buses.
The temperature was admired, the haze beheld.
On a mosaic coaster, an iced coffee perspired by false yellow flowers unblown
by real winds. Kids roamed alone.
Bubbles appeared in the park as bells began.
The utter quaintness! The sense of neighborhood, safety.
The tree: lime-green in that once twilight, stood
there
(that humid night) across the street becoming forest green
and arrived, in darkness, at imperceptibility.
The haze, though, *was*.
The haze
was the underlying beauty of the evening song.
Store lights secured nightly dominance over what was puny daylight.
Sighs were expressed at this resolution.
Rushlights quivered on green-curtained window sills.
Summer winds proceeded to die at the mouth of Buram mountain.
In the park, a man finished a book by Teju Cole, content with his Monday for a
change.
Near a patio, in warmth, by pedestrians fortunate with mesmerism, in the pres-
ence of Buram,
in such an evening haze that bordered fog, the skinny tree with sharp green
leaves
absorbed singularity as a green bus and an orange taxi passed beneath.
Through that (once-beheld) haze, women on phones did walk
under sharp leaflets and branches
held
by ivory crickets breathing.

ACID RAIN DISPOSITION

Through the humid, funereal morn is acid rain upon Gangnam.
While you were sleeping
    the rain slid through dark venom skies
somehow
coming to an end at our window.
Seoul comes to darker shades.
The coffee drip in Café Bene comes to a lull.
The rain grows.
The monks on Buramsan think nothing
of it.
    It's only raining. Some city birds sing.

IN THE SUNLIGHT ON BURAM MOUNTAIN 불암산

Near the summit of a small, steep mountain
squats a ramen and makgeolli vendor, drunk
but deep,
in meditative smile, miles
above all city churches

WATCHING THE NIGHT HIKERS FROM ERIK'S FAR-OFF PORCH

Lantern lights on Sangye's mountain bounce
down the mountain of tanning foreigners
which becomes the mountain of night-hikers
tripping on trails dusted in darkness beneath stolid trees.
I've walked those trails before
felt their mosquitoes and dodged poison ivy,
watched in awe the badminton players
and drank my fair share of makgeolli
(enough to kill a small family of five).
I've been hit
by the resonance of mountainside church bells, so yes
of night-hikes, soju, ramen, and pajeon
I know a bit.
There they go: without haste, laughing nightbreeze, coughing moonlight.
Drunken summer hikes take time,
theirs and ours.

WILD CAT AT 9 P.M.

Wild cat at 9 p.m.
    in a pond of blood-red leaves.
I'm drinking beer in this dark park.
A car parked at the red light plays *Blood on The Tracks*.

III

New England II

SAFE HAVEN

The coming summer promises baseball games
and ablation. Mosquitoes will mate
while potcakes are walked on coastal paths.
Green trees will continue to sigh among haze.
The paperboy will go to college.
A tragedy will convert his apathy to patriotism.
The buzz of a coming election will reach uncharted peaks.
We will forfeit wild nights in the city for quiet beers
to be had in the sanctuary
of a relative's warm, dim den,
temporary respite.
I'm thinking of it all now.
It will be quite forgettable.

QUIET HOUR

The first hard rain of the year shatters the jade leaves.
An hour of muted mirth ensues.
By the window, coffee drips
promises.
Such noises sequester us
from great disasters.
A deer passes through the wet garden
its tail spastic
in the mist
and abyss.

RESOLVES AT TWENTY-FIVE
RESOLVED AT THIRTY-FIVE

Let's not call into question or call attention to my mid-20s imperfections.

I will not risk kids, do not wish to commission a family, cannot trust the world to preserve one.

I will only read in the sun, be done,

and set-off on a series of one-year dreams

relieved by half-year solitudes.

Someday, a stray dog will grow large and loyal.

Not today. Tomorrow is young.

Renewed, I shall read in the sun.

Tonight, I am nude, sober.

There's a party for every Saturday, if sought.

I abstain these days

only read, alone

in Rockport or Portsmouth

stopping to watch only the Celtics

and occasionally make more coffee.

True, time may someday beg pursuit of a partner, perhaps

on an improbable afternoon of solitude and sun, as offered today.

IN HARBORSIDE BARLIGHT

A grayed, frayed barfly author rewrites an opus pocus as rain comes to a soft symphony landing on sidewalk trash bags. A bouncer begs the bikers and hikers to shut down an inebriated showdown at the jukebox. It is possible to play Motown, then indie rock, then classic rock. This resolve spawns happy yawns in the red smoke, and a satisfying denouement settles on the crowd. Tonight, everyone left is leaving, or has already laughed.

CANNOT REMEMBER

Little dogs perfect at the foot of the bed, tail-end of youth
breathing morningtime love, New England air.
I've forgotten our evening song. I've nearly forgotten
everything about blankets and soft whisper meditations
one day to weep, blink, or sleep away
over-think that day
the little black panther
you called a cat
named Huey
ran off into Willard's Woods forever.

DRIVING TO ADK TO CRASH THE
KOZOWSKI 4TH OF JULY

a consciousness in union with the past unites us

on this ride from the Berkshires to the Adirondacks

to see Erik and Andy, who are likely already drunk,

(haven't seen them since Seoul, 2016)

this union with the past is tangible

so, in fact, it does not feel like 2017

what feels is: Present, like 1946

my grandfather

in Woolworth's

buying a comb before his blind date with Joan Fitzgerald.

the slick afternoon sun around summer hot hills and winding pavement

while my father leaps over waves on Martha's Vineyard the summer *Jaws* was released,

like ma reading in musty Amherst stacks for ten minutes, formerly 1983, before dinner,

or Emily down the street simultaneously closing her closet door, but

what are we all doing now? What were we doing before this? Could we be considering

each other across the way, the void, the gap?

the fog is something else nowadays, but it shrouded us then and made one think

of potential names for a baby, or a dog, in union with the past, in the waves of Martha's Vineyard summer *Jaws* was released, worrying

and proving to one another that it isn't all that scary.

the fog, the water

is really quite something, and nothing

to fear.

PORTSMOUTH DAY

Summer porches and obscure gardens!
Breezes sweep the damned heat off porches like dust.
The farmer's almanac instructs
to plant by night
in the light
of the selenotrope moon
by my dog, more noble and gnostic than any of Old Rome's idiots.

THIS SHIT TOWN

is the perfect place to retreat and watch America happen
to see cottages, waterside, present day Portsmouth,
Pray St serving lobster, chowder, wine
and cheese, isolated and too conscious of magnolia petals
falling by the bucolic second
ah any fleeting thing, amendment to
all the historic wooden houses downtown
(built by/for 19th century craftsmen, carpenters, fishermen, painters)
will not make it. They, too, fall soon.

DID THE DOG JUST MAKE THAT NOISE?

I slept for thirteen hours again,
twelve in this bed. Still tired.
Will I ever live in Lowell? I long. You yearn.
New York? The hills? Buenos? Move back to Seoul?
Or, will I just stay, lay
here an hour more
perhaps die in that hour
rushing, longing, desiring a longer time.
I have not paid my bills for ages, speaking of time.
    Come and get me.

SAME: KILIM COFFEE WALK IN THE SNOW

To pass sickness sinking in, I watched an expensive parked car get hit.
The driver ran. Good.

Snowing harder now.
Hopefully tomorrow night I can drink and accomplish everything on earth
twice.

The people across the road may think I'm staring at them; I'm simply appreciating
the snowfall. Yesterday it was 75 degrees. Been drunk five of the last seven days.

Such habits happen in New England homes when it snows. Evening dawns.
The neighbors are closer in proximity than they used to be

but we're miles apart as a community.
Looks like it could be the last snowfall, again.

Solitude distraction attention snow cider hermitude piano key
Light from inside drifts

to the wet street outside
disturbed

but
compromising.

Am I a child
for acting this way?

WINTER SCENE

New Year's Day below zero
dark resolutions abound
caucasians on the chalked sidewalk
trees too frozen to shiver
two-chimney houses and Sir Patrick's school in the setting sun

This isn't New York; it's Portsmouth
Irish gargoyles gargle sunlight over a stoic yellow house
at last! a snowy park full of dog prints
icicles full of daytime, too cold to melt
snow blows smooth over a field, a leaf is stuck
then moves, like the chipmunk monk
in search of who knows
but seeking, seeking
sneaking home
from the wildlife penury
but seeking

CURRIER AND IVES

The snow rhymes
   with the
rustic New England winter scene.
An 1832 silent, unmoving brown house
in which two spouses fuck.

(YOUR SNOWSTORM MORNING LIPS)

    three coffee pots by noon
not enough coffee in the world to make enough time
    to work, love, and sleep
by the fire—all the elements
    small house with attractive coffee
wind-blown intent
    I went out and played in the snow
made forts in the bushes like a kid
    You stayed in
plaid, two button underwear
    reading one of ninety-four books with "*The Girl. . .*" in the title
I asked you what it meant
    You said another day
had passed us by

PORTSMOUTH_IV

Evening: Begin.
    three chur*hes toll bells without harm or harmony
    this is the right time to return home from walks
    when the sun docks behind the brewery and ill winds rise
    or time arises to take the dog to the park behind the makeshift graveyard
    as a sharp breeze raises the consciousness of dormant nipples

    who knew bamboo could grow here
    at the back of this field?
    an evening so red, one might not rise from slumber ever again

    but happy hours do flourish
    and you have not missed one in years
    and beauty
    is a fleeting sip of a cloudy drink

    it rained last week. will rain again.
    water lilies appear near the dock, all occasions must end
    but an artist ignores such atrocities (strains to strain)
    the floating thin taunt of summer curtains over a couch
    like homemade latte foam (Buenos Aires mug) oh
    just to watch thunderstorms with you
    when summer suddenly strikes April

CABOT ST. MARKET WHEN IT'S POURING

cashier's smoke-break silence
some familiar words: *lull, pause, peace, quietude*
beatitude. cloud-dark store windows and
an encroaching, sinister formation above.
peace in such heat, the clerk, the empty store,
he and his thoughts of torrential rain
down an empty isle staring, moment of being, half-remembering
a six pack
back home in the attic mini fridge

APRIL FOOLS; NOT WHAT NO ONE TALKS ABOUT

The apple is
among other qualities
quite exquisitely illiterate.
Snow is
what disrupts the highway
pollution. The highway destroyed
our neighborhood half-a-century ago
but no one talks of that anymore
no more than they do the score of fires
concealed in Gloucester's past, Gloucester
where the limp fish, sideways-peering, smile
plump-full of ice.
April Fools, not
what no one talks about
among other
quite exquisitely illiterate things: Snow.
The snow disrupts highway
pollution. The highway displaced
our neighborhood half-a-century ago
but no one talks of that any more
than they do the scores of fires
concealed in Gloucester's history.

I'M A PART OF THE NIGHT

Tonight, in houses near people, break routine.
I don't know. I'm here alone with my oldest coyotito dog.
The house behind me either has family over,
or their house has fallen over
and I'm here, wine drunk reading Eli and Pro-
crastinating. Ah, summer will begin now
and soon Rockport will have its ways.

I used to desire downtowns on a night like this
but I like more the thought
of them
down there
and me, up here
with a solitary light,
wasting.

BERKSHIRES RETURN

We went to Willie's
to get keys from Eli
who had told Willie of me at Meg's (ma of Carlo)
home earlier. Eli would soon join us at the home of Miles.
All these names are real. Mine is Max
to prove it. Liz and Patrick
stood quiet by the car, all of us
on this dark side of a moonlit mountain. Next morning, a dog followed Naomi's
friend into the home and licked me
awake to learn the smell and taste of hangover, as Mudge,
the cat, watched. There were nameless
spiders thin and eager over the toilette which Naomi
had named Lee.

WITHOUT A FORGOTTEN LINE

still life, life still as March's
mid-storm grocery stores.
stories are lost in harbor bells.
just what is it Rockport
in which all my failure has led me to you?
why has Gloucester a ferrini mural and nothing of olson (lie)
nothing of garbo, eliot, nothing of its real past, as it shifts into
white collar vacation lore
like the other cape?
what is the name of the fullness of this moon?

three days from now
meet me in the town square by the Neck.
i'll dress in black so the snow shows.
we'll sit on the harbor bench and watch the world at sea
and pretend the world snows all at once
as we breathe, filling the cold ether
til covered in snow, eyeing the harbor,
wishing our hands weren't gloved,
suspecting seagulls somewhere in the thickness above
racing rapturously through such symmetry
of falling flakes which end in or as harbor water
or as the thing which erases imprints of soles.
we could sit on the torn harbor floor instead
where moonlight melts snow
and, or we could leave solitude behind
as the world curdles in front of us,
one seaside city at a time.

DEBRIS BY THE TRACKS

a body,

some cans, some glass,

a kilim, a bumble bee inspecting scraps, maps of trails,

the tail of a flattened rat, feces, a sudden cat, items bought once with cash (tales of trash),

lumber, more glass, a "no trespass railroad police" sign.

You Don't Have To Explain Shit To Anyone.

K.

Pangs. Knowing. (Radiance).
To be alive with you in London, 1838.
Where? Cold hotels.
On poetic notions. In shafts of light. By sharp park benches.
Our hearts are ancient friends. You're in Athens
but I still see you
over my left shoulder.
You cannot know
how I once went through Seoul
on three occasions however insignificant.
I cannot know how you felt in Buenos Aires
minutes before waking,
gently inhaling the good air.
Argentina it is.

IN ROCKPORT'S LAST LIGHT, EVENING
IS PALPABLE, HAS BREATH.

I see the people breathing, writhing
    in the dim colors of Feather and Wedge
    behind the old harbor, indistinct in the night.
The seagulls along the ledge teeter,
    ocean dark as hills in Dakota.

Too cold for the vets to converse at the head of Bearskin Neck.
Too cold for the cats to come out from under the library steps.

On Dock Square, where the tree stands, where the trolley stops, where the ball drops,
    where people in sun once scurried, continent's edge,
    the cafes are closed, stores snowed-in for the season.
Artists have fled, but bookish folk sit engrossed in story by lamps.

To belong here is to resign, to submit. But
what if one remembers
    how alive and unforgiving
    that dark harbor did move
    Motif No.1
    ebbing and laughing in the, well, never mind.

www.ingramcontent.com/pod-product-compliance
Lightning Source LLC
LaVergne TN
LVHW051707080426
835511LV00017B/2781